DEATH STYLES

DEATH STYLES

JOYELLE MCSWEENEY

NIGHTBOAT BOOKS

NEW YORK

ISBN: 978-1-643-62230-9

Cover design and interior typesetting by Kit Schluter
Typeset in Italian Old Style MT

Thanks to Robin Myers for translating
Dolore Dorantes's words about *Death Styles*.

Cataloging-in-publication data is available
from the Library of Congress

Nightboat Books
New York
www.nightboat.org

CONTENTS

DEATH STYLES

for my daughters

8.11.20

A SKUNK

It's dawn and I'm out in the grey-green light with the dog.

Dawn is also a style: black Vans and a Marimekko robe,

the most expensive thing I own.

I cinch it with a slash and feel glamorous.

The leash is also a style.

The dog in her spotted sheath is also style.

I cross the field beside the tennis courts

where the high school boys meet for trust exercises

laced in each other's arms before the net.

Everything is laced together

& nothing drains away,

nothing drains away.

But does it have to be this beautiful.

Madder stops the storm drain.

Wet grass knots at my feet

I hate it, no I like it. No, I like it

as I kick my way to the sidewalk, sneakers soaked

above their trademarked rubber soles,

a loneliness American as a kick in the teeth.

Weeds disapprove of this remark and lean away,

the dog goes along 'reading her novel,'

some other creature's mark or waste.

I remember one morning where

one early morning where

a skunk was crossing a large, groomed lawn

shielding his head with his spread tail

also large, groomed, and dazzling as any canopy raised

to shield a crown or cargo bay

in Ancient Egypt or in space

by astronauts—their tools, their formal pace.

How like a coin the skunk turns on his edge to show his profile

Is it my slingshot or my birdbrain

my predator or my prey

my lunar or my earthly style

that right now freezes me in place.

The radio detective says, "Aye, it's a planet of killers,"

and I'm another

and the skunk is another

improbable king

masking a killer

gnomon and antonym

or vice versa

The skunk made a diamond of the lawn with his diagonal path

my husband wanted to watch

I wanted to leave, afraid to be sprayed

but really afraid of his magnificent shape

magnificently

self-contained

that can stand on its head on the equator like an egg

or split its own brain with its own secateurs

in two equal hemispheres

and execute

any move

under that moon

-walk: sock of white, glove of white

sidewalk that lights

all times are noon

I want to live in that

microregime which

pulls the watchface

all around itself

black eye that winks back

from the center of the watch

where the hands should be attached

but the hands are gone

the watchface is blank

the style

points exactly to itself

shoves both mickey mouse gloves in its mouth

it never leaves home

but takes any long spear of shadow

directly into its eye

and swallows it up

to stop it traveling

no time passes

but you can stay forever

if you agree to block out your eyes

go anaerobic

and give everything else up

a mesh and two drains

a distended abdomen

a nudge and wink

a little half grin

and a little flexing arm

all signs of infant seizure

but only in one picture

can you see her mouth make

that shape that makes me shake

and I've deleted that photo anyway

I've deleted the photon

shoved it right back up the gut

of the cosmos that made it

and sent it shooting out across universe

going the wrong way

—you're going the wrong way!

—what? how do you know where we're going?

I mouth the dialogue

I put my thumb in my mouth to mime the drinking

I will do at five o'clock

on the dot

at the spot

in the center of the clock

face, watch face, sundial, style

we put the gel in her hair

for the EEG

then decided to scrap the test

so she died with her black hair gunky

I hate that

where were we when

I hate that

where were we when

I don't hold her

because I don't want to hurt her while she dies

or after

because she feels so much

more dead and heavier

anyway

where were we

when we watched that skunk cross that diamond

when he turned in profile

and made a procession of himself

entailed a retinue

raised his million-dollar solar shade

and shot himself out of all this trouble

all the gauges shake and gag as he

points to the stands

hits a grand slam

& rides the diamond right up into the banks of light above the
stadium

and then beyond

so bright

the camera cannot follow him

up there where

we could hold our breath and

go anaerobic but are dismayed to be

denied entry

to the tomb

our mortal bloodstreams

flood with waste

the brainalarms sound

and all the green numbers roll back in their heads

we're forced to take a breath

and I would take

any accelerant or suppressant

slick down my pulse like an infant's cowlick

run my heart down like a medieval town clock

a stuck gory orgy of moral urges

there the maiden studies her reflection in the apple

the miller stops beating his wheat

the bird seeks to dislodge the song from its throat

or else whack my heart off till it beats

so hard it shakes loose from the cage and flees

the red-stained drain cool tile and golden hook where I

hang myself up like a hotel robe

& anaerobe

back to where

we were when we

stopped

at the sight of the skunk

before the green that rose

& sharpened our sight

on that diamond

8.13.20

To circle is also a style.

The temple has a door—but where is it?

Most of the time you just stay home and roll around in the
madder. You roll with your back in the madder. This is some-
thing you learned from the dog. To take things in through your
spine. To wear your knowledge on your pelt. Most of the time,
you stay in and drink your liquid wings. You try to train the
baby to watch television. The bottle is clear as a chrysalis with
something stirring and forming inside.

The dog survived pregnant in the woods for some months,
lonely and semiferal. She who needs to be accompanied now
to eat from her clean bowl. Her age, her breed, her provenance,
who puppy trained her then turned her out into the Tennessee
woods for the most primal of adventures, no one can say. How
she withstood it. Obviously she is a woman.

She has no desire to reveal her name or her parentage or escape
her fosterage to return as the hero. She firmly rejects the role.

An interview with the TV detective: how he lost his accent and
got a TV accent.

But still cannot say the phrase "world of murderers" so takes for
his catchphrase "planet of killers."

When he finds the door he will need a device to jimmy it open.
A credit card, a gemmy wrench, a charm of words. Or else just
knock it open with a bar.

That gemmy, wrenching feeling as the planet turns away from you.

The comet is up there somewhere behind the crowds and you're
missing it. You're messing it up.

You don't know where the baby is. The detective is on the case. You want to sleep in the parking lot outside the funeral home.

Your fingers in (the comet's) jammy hair.

You're the grieving mother and you're helping the detective. You run a finger down the column of inked figures. All the guilt is there. Tiny beetles are working away at the glue. After the baby dies you are all struck with lice. Your daughter asks you, Why do I have lice? You answer, Dunno, why anything, why did the baby die, as you comb away the lice. There's always more of them. You run a fever down the seam of the book and split it with your fingernail and tear the page away. To hide your theft you expectorate.

You let it off your chest.

On the job you wear a hatband tilted like a ring of Saturn. You may only be viewed in three-quarter view as you study the titles, loans, lots, deeds, and water tables in the Bureau of Records. The ceilings are high with a row of windows for harpies to peer in but the air feels soupy as a nest of meat. But everyone comes to the Bureau of Records. A very glamorous place!

You sit at the picnic table where the groundsmen take their lunch breaks to interview the priest. The priest attempts a casual demeanor, like he could take it or leave it. He wears a dog collar. There is a problem between you and the priest but he circles around it.

You return to the hall of records to pick up her birth cert. You must check a box to collect the birth cert of a decedent.

O ancestor I object.

Why did you choose this life for us.

You circle what looks like an equipment shed but is actually a chapel. From the outside it feels like a replica. You circle it like a dog to find the entrance. Feel your hands cup into claws. Finally you are on your knees crawling up the steps of the chapel.

You are deafened by a deafening regret. Your hearing was going somewhere and then it went. Your lips curl in all the irony, because of its acrid smell.

Like what-do-you-call-it: Balmex. Carmex.

What they put on the pharaoh's lips: a scarab.

A bombilation.

You enter the chapel. Of course it's odorless. And at the center of the altar stands a white box.

It's too small. Too pitiably small. The true galactic feeling of the galaxy-as-sea goes rocking around the room. The chapel tips like a ship. We're landlocked, I want the sea to rush from its lunar occipitals and rock to back flood the skull. Drown all this, and that, or also, lift this away, and that, too, thanks. Pitch it elsewhere.

You want this. You do.

As the feathers drifted down from the exploded hull, it began to dawn on the crew of the spacecraft how life proceeds by error, not by plan.

It began to dawn on the crew of the life raft.

(The rats don't make mistakes.)

It began to dawn on Planet Killer.

At the end of the day the groundskeepers speed away from the cemetery, as from any other job. But you plan to sleep here, in the diggers' shed

crawl down to her grave and lay on the blades

your hundred sticky eggs

8.14.20

R I V E R   P H O E N I X

What I'm waiting for: someone to shout instructions from the sky

through some barely imaginable instrument.

I've cleared out all my hearing for this

but no voice comes. I'm hiding in the tiny yard because I'm
thronged with people, laundry, dishes, subfunctional computer
equipment, weeds, animals, mold, and a virus wrapped around
the planet like a tumor wrapped in veins. It should be exciting
but it's dank as a cape.

What I want is to be snatched out of this place.

In the theater of my brain I run the blockbuster. You're a pro-
fessor, archaeologist, and detective, a bad mentor. In the opening
scenes you teach inside a rolltop desk. I see myself in you when
your hair is disarranged to indicate disbelief and incomprehen-
sion, something rolling from the sky. Comprehension arrives
like a boulder, train, snake, soda siphon, lady in diaphanous dress
or wrapped in cellophane, secondary racist caricature. Even a
child has to make his face plain for you to read it.

For a scholar you are dumb.

But then, love's dumb as a spoon, hate's both a dull blade and a
sharp one. Eat up

with your baby spoon and your baby blade.

Both you and me wear a bob, but when you are a man it is
blond.

I want another baby to waste my time on. To stuff its mouth
with my time. To unreel that eternal Bataillean matinee....

I could pick up the phone and...

some unfortunate...

Forget the movies.

I am having an at-home experience.

Beauty regimes, cleaning regimes: I have none of these.

I sit in the backyard and evade my re-spons-i-bilitees

...but this is also fantasy. In fact I spend hours on the phone convincing AT&T to beam their signals into our house, and also to take our signal out again, up to their unimaginable servers. I bribe them with time, humor, money, nothing works. It's like one of those gas heaters in a British spy novel: each morning I wake to feed the slot with coins.

I'm having a hard time with the celebrity baby news on the Internet today. Because I am an idiot. And the babies of celebrities do not die? Or they have enough monee and time to keep trying

till one stays all day.

The backyard is just a skinny nub of lot and it's grown with weeds like where they found the Black Dahlia.

I'm on hold, so I have time to daydream and read abstruse texts.

It's like the old medieval joke about the miller, his daughter, and the comet that crashed through, incinerating everything.

What did you name her. What was her name.

Back to the movie: there's a young man trailing behind you on a train and it's River Phoenix.

He's another blond, your son, lover or double, and no matter how many times you cut the bolt or flip the switch like a dream he still hangs on.

I'm tired of this scene. And I don't want none of it

—except the bob and River Phoenix.

"Like a dream he still hangs on."

8.17.20

LEONARD COHEN, CLYTEMNESTRA

Surely I am evading my responsibilities:

hiding out in the backyard, choosing to believe

my teens are working/learning when they are

pursuing their own privacy on the Internet

like nymphs gathering blooms in a bright field above a seam

bird-eye ticks at the bottom of the well

and won't give back even light

it wants to blink

wants to rub its own eye

and go to sleep

in the seam of itself

I want something pulled out of me

like a maiden witched back up out of the well

or maybe I want

to sit and blink at the bottom of it

let the heir tumble into me

live forever there

dead and romantic

well that's one way to do it

become a holy well

in the holy see

in the middle of the night

we watch 8 mm films about the island of Hydra

an island named for water

as if to hide itself in its name

in its own open eye

there Leonard and Marianne swim and swim

as if the water itself

is the island of Hydra

eviscerating itself

in clear alcohol

ouzo and ozone

I need that operation

to take the ache out

a useless instrument left there by a god

a brass instrument with a knot in its middle

also left there by a god

but that's just fantasy

I need no operation

on that parody Elysium

I tote around

ancient huntresses went around in holy girdles

ancient matrons whipped out their breasts

in a fervor, ripped up their sons

with their seamrippers

snip snip went the seam

between temperance, intemperance

they invented tragedy

then hurled the whole world through it

a periphery perforated by

absurdity and calamity

like funeral games performed for a slain infant

where the victor wins a crown of celery

If you are going to wear a crown, it should be made of something

ridiculous, that bobs

I take this lesson to heart

when I imagine we meet at the bottom of the sea

and you are something pollen-like and flourishing in the nitrogen seams

and I grub around with comically distended jaws

dismayed by so much gravity and

bearing a fleshy bauble pedunculating from my brow

nearby

like the watchfire on Mount Arachne

in Aeschylus's Agamemnon

lit up second-to-last

before the bad news comes crashing home

to run the murder-bath

as like a jerk

I jerk about in the bird bath

trying to focus the world's image

in each of my four foveae

as time flies by on jerk's wings

and my alarm clock brain keeps slotting, slotting

through all the devotional hours of the day

I have to jerk my head to one side

I have to slit my eyes

I have to look at it

sidewise

like a pencil rolling under the desk

byebye

when I receive a phone call

from a gentleman named Spam Risk

who resides in Black Eddy, Pennsylvania,

I do not answer it

8.18.20

Why don't you rinse your blonde child's hair in dead champagne to keep it gold, as they do in France?

Why don't you have every room done up in every color green? This will take months, years, to collect, but it will be delightful—a mélange of plants, green glass, green porcelains, and furniture covered in sad greens, gay greens, clear, faded and poison greens?

—DIANA VREELAND, HARPER'S BAZAAR

Why don't you

stand before the door

black bows on your wrists

in one of two identical pairs of shoes

this one with rubber soles for wet days

any cobbler can do this

why don't you

palm frond, breadmold, emerald, seabladder,

filing cabinet, verdigris, eau du Nil—

this morning I stood before the door

I studied it like a riddle

the riddle was: When did I forget how to open doors

I carry a ring of keys like Bluebeard's bride

beerbottle, greengage, keylime

it is always tugging down my pockets

except when I wear a denim jacket!

with little rivets

that sing like birds in the eye

the keys are looking smaller than they did before

another riddle

21

each one intricate and baffling

I look closer and one bears the profile of the Royal Pavilion in
Brighton

even smaller that it did before

when i used to go there

i wore a half-slip for a skirt and my hair in artful knots

as memory hooks on to memory

the cortex darts with pins and knots

the doorknob is replaced with a skyknob

something like the handle on a tankard

but how do you turn a key in a mug

or turn the key in the sky

of course eventually i shove with my shoulder

and tumble into the house to do my chores

how can you

why don't you

in order to better concentrate

i decide to buy the milk later in the day

to clear time to write and now all i think about is milk

milk milk

i crawl all over the house looking for dirty bottles

rubber nipples and plastic collars

"like nebuchadnezzar"

i set em in the sink to further rot

mid-morning sun ticks across

the royal pavilion at brighton

a pier gently rots into the sea

and throws off a gas which heats the sky

when i was there

nothing but a half slip between me and the pier

and, contrariwise, my blackest, heaviest shoes,

a pigeon rotted rudely, exposing its chest

a fish rots from the head and a bird from the chest

quoth the pigeon

who were dead

what were being diagram'd there

above the pier

the vampire's house

rose skinny as himself and his bride

shouldering twin sons

one of whom would later fall to his death

from millstone to millstone

where the sea grinds the cliff

then they flew off to LA

why don't you

move to LA

traipse along a catwalk

above the sign

that tells you where you are

wash your face in it

why don't you

wash your dead child's face in champagne

i did wash her face in blonde

no more tears baby shampoo

to release the residue of tape

when it was too late

I had already learned the scent of her: a shock

of alcohol that shook the brain

like priests and goblins shake the pews with censers

scrabbling up the aisle toward the altar

there to deposit our eyes

but will we ever arrive

every thirty days i

receive a text from apple

urging me to delete the images

that eat my memory up

delete them, or I will

says the apple

I won't

i have my own

pursuits

i have my own

evil routes

i learned from reading a burning book

in a burning library

while the baby was alive

& J sang

the factory is closed

let's go to venice

i'll dress you in white denim

with rivets to sing

i made that last part up

je voudrais

aller à venise

and i would like

to sing it now

i'm singing it now

from the lip

of the throat-decaying pier

you can hear it

wing into the air

baby's breath

on every sanitized hand

look angel:

pass over, or don't

i don't care

i'll just stand here on the threshold

feel the wind you bear in your ratwings

rinse my hair

i can't find the door

i can't open it

i can't remember how doors work

blow the house down

eat the door

green buckle, green udder

green that freckles the gravestones

eats the carbon diox

with green teeth

chlorophyll endorphin

ebony green

as weeds in the gutter

wave from the second floor

why

why don't you

claim every green as yours

8.19.20

ANGER, KRATER

When I say I have a face of anger
When I say I have an anger face
this specifically female problem
clarifies the self-gaze
and functions like a mirror
held up by a fledgling boy
humiliating problems
draw humiliating answers
mix the wine in a krater
with honey, spice, or water
odd numbered days are easier to survive
the odd-faced coin rolls slower
till it finally falls over
into some flaw in the floor
and is gone into the ether
can I imagine a frictionless space
shower of sugar
cold as it is hot
where I'm fastening my custom Cousteau-mask
onto my linen suit
and readying for my spacewalk
to be assassinated by the plot
what's my line chop't
like a heroic bob
on the cutting room floor

eject me now into the Polaroid darkness

I'm ready to go

the doors won't open/close

there's a leak in the suit/tank/hose

my learning is stuffed up in mine helmet

mine Internet

has a crack in it

when I pose on air I take a step forward

a smile cracks my face

just like on an attic vase

this is to indicate I am opposite a horizon

and gazing upon it:

the future

like when the hairdresser undoes the foil to watch the color lift

from black shafts, and the yellow odor drapes the room

and makes every curler, every curled-lip lift:

the future

maybe she's born with it

the kosmos is littered with Ancient Greeks

how they imagined things

stepping in and out of the bathtub

trying to understand it

looking around for a lever

trying to stand outside of it

filling their mouths with rock

because it's easier

than finding an honest person

like our toddler cries because he wants two things

and only has one mouth

I hit snooze

and pull the lips of the iris close

stop up the conch shell

whatever tomb's willing to house me

I seal myself up in it

still, bad news litters the loom

when the dog kills a house mouse bloodlessly

it curls up so decoratively

I can barely discern it

from the pattern in the rug

now everything flicks like the tail of the mouse

in the corner of my eye

and my crooked part

which one morning went pale with shock

is now black and greasy again

like the place where two seas meet

Greek guards push migrants back onto the sea

having first disabled their motors

leave them there to drift or drown

the Lady of Shalott glances at the dumb world in her mirror

and then decides to drown in it

the brass rooster tucked

by the shoulder of the toddler

in its grave beneath the carpark

you brought it up

now put it back

with your betty page bangs and rumpled collar

with your chignons or updos that snare and break the necks
of men

toss the driver from the cart

reinstall the driver

throw your baby in the pot

and take him out again

with a prosthetic shoulder

that no longer does that seizing thing

that freekd you out

and ruined your good looks and your good luck

what you would like to have in your mouth

is gone

along

with the word for it

snap your jaws back

light a fire

boil your brain with your rage

your skull for a krater

the gods those sick mothers

pushed the mortals onto the face of the sea

after first disabling the motors

left them to drift and die

in a bowl burnt blue burnt black

and the gods aren't good enough

for the offerings we have made to them

take it back

8.21.20

A LIE DETESTOR FOR MATTHEW RHYS

Now it is time to

learn a new alphabet

Not drinking is for pregnant women

you're not pregnant

just a little green

so drink up, baby

like a nymph or mantic dream

the alcohol evaporates before it hits the back of your throat

makes your vision better

of that boy who stood in a garden in sock garters

like the stylus in a dial, looking up

and died early of a heart problem

beat the clock

he still stands undiagnosed in his summer allotment

no rose rotates under him

but when I water him with gin

our summer returns through the holes in the speakers

just a little green

around the edges

something I don't want to see

speeds by in the corner of my eye

the current blips

the struggling AC complains superiorly

the detective next to me in the jalopy

looks kind of dented

like folding money, a straw

or the stylus of an early audiograph

tuning the toothmarked fossil record

into a summer sweet wine

when I peek sidelong I see a daffodilic nimbus

rise tentatively around him

a hibiscoid nimbus

half collar half veil

whoa

go ovoid

wow

husks like it might be plush to touch

I can still see him through it

passed out, gone some other place

can it be simple as that

and silly

half or less than half awake

and still profound

hoosier adoration of trampolines

hazard insurance neckbrace

all the rising and sinking

gradual and violent shaking

the mist the goddess conceals her son in

when she yanks him out of battle

then reverses

to toss him back into the day

he lost weight for this role

and his skin is pea-hued

you'll never get pre

gnant like that

and you'll never get a pre

approved

loan

again

smashed up on a windscreen

bent like a stovepipe

thrown down the drainpipe

a banged-up memory-storage device

each time we hit a pothole, my chassis

convulses, the detective

so dry at the joint

he clanks

could make a new lie detestor

by strapping himself to the bed

this is a dry county

therefore it is imperative we cross over the line into the next one

when I am in Texarkana /where's the county line

goes a song that exists only in demo

I like it for how it's going no place

for the audible way it's falling apart

like the detective's fish-green neck

sends up a tentative odor

I'm drawn to like a god-dog

the taint

of accelerated

posthumicity

that only mortals possess

as they race decay to death

the dream of dying perfect

that's the dream

we're all in together

me and this boy and the detective and my car

I'll have paid off

in eight year's time oh

Art

go off somewhere I'm busy

go solve a crime

8.24.20

To pull the brown corduroy skirt around myself like a cape and
open the door

To cover every surface with fur

It seems as a child I was always dressed in capes

aquamarine hoods

red knit capelets

with my own girls I forgot to do this

but their grandmothers both remembered

so we can do the wolf scene

on both sides

To wear a man's cotton undershirt

and zip myself into the stiffest of jeans

and eat by halves

and never be done eating

seeds and nuts

rinds and husks

down the gullet

normal love

great pasty triumph

rise and fall of Rose Green Horror

to descend the pink stucco apartment with my airhounds to
meet my lover

to crash the jalop into the lot at LAX

to let a thousand dahlias bloom from my ribcage

35

or escape on slippery hooves

the red velvet rope around the abattoir

chinstrapped in a bellhop's toque trimmed with a bell

plus ça ring bell plus c'est même chose

says the gulp of wasps from their magasin

they have all the best diacriticals

and they keep them for themselves

<<don't blame your shitty French on the wasps>>

ding dong down all the streets with all the deaths

me and my flock

but also we take a beating to the crown

the little wasp hands strike and pound

the little guy with the clawhammer

alarms the clockface so delirium tremendously

he cannot advance the plot

I drink a lot but my hand is steady

possibly because I drink from flutes

modeled on the daffodil larynx

this film is constantly edited down to be flushable

but rise again to swamp the drains with multiples

a luxury everyone can afford

like that pink liquid soap in public bathrooms

pump your own

a tomb, a casino, and a soap called "luxor"

lather generously up

under the stars' spread-eagle

pink-spangled circus tent

puff up your chest

and ride the neck of the escalator

up to the glass roof of the emporia

where they use to serve snacks

before the goddess Luxuria took on too much debt

and foundered

it's going to reopen as a penthouse cum health club

a crease known only to wealth

but you can visit there

if you know how to clean

with my luggage and this plumage I arrive too late

at the platform and have to set out walking

I tote my embassy thusly into the dark

tunnel over and tunnel under

drag regal seal and sealskin

robe so stiff I can barely eke

the line out at my throat

the channel's overrun with eyesores today

everyone's confinement trophies

sonograms and matted lanugo hair

glamorous exhaustion comes in all colors

the lilacs too burnt to bloom

glower all summer

and crumble when someone brushes against them

suet left for the birds in its special black cage

is eaten before it can rot

croak, monsieur

or croak, madame

so called because an egg is smashed there

as bombs improve a cathedral

a perforated clinic

lets in more light

the tumor is morcellated

and the hair marcelled

when the nurses pull out the instruments

they sing a counting song

so nothing is forgotten

every scalpel, every clamp

knows its place on the cart

clip clip

goes the hairdresser

in the basement of the depart

-ment store   it's going to rain today

but you won't feel a thing where you're going

8.25.20

HOSPITAL PLANTERS

I'm sorry you had to throw away the new earthenware cup

and all the natural-fiber clothes you bought at the men's store
on the corner

for bearing the taint of men's

purple auras

mauveine, synthesized by some undergrad trying to make quinine

and fuchsine, later renamed after the battle of Magenta,

Mauveine, fuchsine, magenta, maybe it were better

you were never born

I'm sorry you never wore the navy blue singlet

we bought to escape from all that baby girl pink

we escaped it all right

even the cartilage on your ears went bent and rigid

as a cartridge

you couldn't bear a secret there

even if you tried

and you tried

I'm sorry for that

sorry we didn't recognize the purpuration of your ankles for the
sign it was

despite the nurse's signals

sorry I got worked up about the sore on your knee and exasper-
ated the nurses

I was afraid it would get infected! Your little knee.

You were just a little fat

I'm sorry we didn't take you out to feel the rain on your face before you died/or after

sorry we didn't take you up on the roof

or out on the breezeway amid the hospital planters

pale concrete things crowned with improbably fragrant grass

a precious scent

like something from the song of solomon

ankle graceful as an ankle strap

kidsole of the comet flashing by

Darling

I'm sorry you didn't survive

reverse aubade

every time the sun rises

I want to crumple up

this whole heliocentric universe

still the helicopter rises from its crumpled cup

outside the hospital down the hill

and I race out toting your foster brother to wave at it

Good bye good bye

come back this time

Knit booties and the eyedropper of a kitten

you revolved in a catball eye

till the skin of the water burst

like the film where they shoot the apple

and its crown drops into the milk

thread a little camera into the uterus

watch what beats there

so glad you came and went before all this badness

of which you were the advent

your name on the parking pass which for some reasons sticks
around

fishing itself back up every so often from the muck in the back
of the hatchback

like a bone in the fish's throat

self-cannibalizing fish

in love enough with itself

to choke on its own bone

a leveret and a loach

go out rowing in a nut

on planet fish

in a Japanese song

I ball my hands together and thrust

like a parody of prayer or wish

just below the sternum

and try to dislodge what's lodged

at the urging of my digital instructor

I'm renewing my foster license

just now I want to live

in the pyramid on the money

inside the eye inside the park

look out from that pinhole camera

at the sphinxes patrolling the New England graves

not telling their secrets

not giving them up

the hospital planters

shake their aromatic heads

in the night

in the sodium light

41

how we petted them, brushed against them like cats

so the scent stuck around in our fur

and emanated a third cat

as we rounded corners, climbed steps

bathroom, balustrade, embankment, berm

all the locks we had to work to get to your berth

like a couple of tomb raiders

infiltrating your sacred chamber

converted to devotees thereafter

trying to live in the tomb

every time we left or returned we met

that oily scent

more amber than lavender

more persistent, more regretful,

more distended, more vengeful

like a cur the scent recurs

drips from its own jaw

like in the movie called 'White God'

the teen goes pedaling in the street

on her way home from orchestra practice

the whole orchestra of curs

rises around her

in that organized way of the weather seen from space

bad thoughts and bad news

a nasal rawness

as if someone had mowed down my frontal cortex

carved your name into my brain

weather and porn feeds loop and revolve

everything needs to be shaved

made barer

mounted again

the vapidity of mammals

the elegance of a riparian

snaking an egg along its length

your blade spins close, spins away

up and over me

as luckier women

stagger the halls held up by balloons

oh get me a beret

to hold my brain in

the creek gotta rise

in the birth canal

in parking structure

in the retaining wall

in the hospital planter

let something rise

then let it fall

no censer no chancre

was ever so bereft

of your scent

8.27.20

DAUGHTER STYLE

Now we have a secret and it's your secret

difficult to keep as the clasp on a vinyl diary

you snap off

when you're angry in your tenth solitude

We love the story about poison daughters

growing in a poison garden

whose kiss would kill the suitors

so don't even try

live with me forever I've changed my mind

I want to take you outside and photograph you among the Rose
of Sharon

still holding on to its good looks

in the narrow, overgrown lot

because its hothouse vibe reminds me of you

and the colors you favor this season

and the lot itself reminds me

there's an opening still

but it's narrow and blocked with weeds

maritime sightlines of the landlocked

middle-aged goth mom mystic

When we wake up for school in the dark

something sick and green is flashing

above the crowns of trees

and behind them

the smoke that trails from fireworks

45

more beautiful than fireworks themselves

hangs around, a glaucous glut

of fist-shaped marled chrysanthemums, the gut

of a middle-aged goth mom mystic

When I open and shut

your drawers, your neat laundry

dawns and dusks:

petal, orchid, baby blue,

flamingo, candy, lavender, dove-hued

galactic dust but pour milk on it

like some revolting nebula

shot in stop-motion and sped up

I lift you up to your loft amid your peach and blue materials

Your father cleans all the ink away with alcohol

In the photograph with your pink mask on

you lift your white-wrapped paws

8.31.20

DAUGHTER STYLE (NORMAL LOVE)

We gather round a blue eye in the stage

I'm fastened into my Levi's

like the last Swan King

who floated off on an ear

and was drowned by a valet

who also drowned

but I lock my ankles in the rushes

and stick around for now

Swans die nightly here

because of the drainage problem

and are fished out of the drains each day

with golden rakes

A dead swan is a fish

just as a limp dick

has begun its journey

out of practicality

and into Elysium

This parable elucidates

today's production: *Normal Love*

The mermaid Death-in-Life

lies half in, half out of the eye

and is played by Mario Montez

who also goes by Réne

and is pursued by a hot satyr

with curls in his eyes

who keeps slipping in the mud

and out of the frame.

When the scene reaches its limp peak

they reject pursuit

whereupon the eye produces

a bottle of Coke

Both drink

    End scene—

but one senses it revolves

and plays again

while we're looking at something else

We have zeal but lack commitment

Our failure inverts to glamour

and re-arrives as the divine

Here comes the unsteady mermaid again

for the lumpy fracas

But our eyes are on the plain maiden

weeping in the potato-peel rain

a flotilla of cysty blimps in Bronco Stadium

or a skinny youth leaning against the Alps

who returns to Memphis, records an album,

then shoots his car into an oak's full crown

O god-in-tree, o maiden, bird

willing to lay its neck down in the rushes

and weave its own basket,

God's Chik-n-biskit, loyal bird...

   ...Today's the day for sweatshirts

but you won't wear one. Your hair's a cherry slick

that hides your face, your socks are cherry mixed

with water and your sneaker tips

a toothy white. You work them in the dirt.

Your ankle tangles in a string.

When you rise up on your kite you ride

and settle in some meadow of your choosing.

9.1.20

DAUGHTER STYLE

So odd like a gun and
has to go off
with you, to unlock the next level
to unlock the drain
to uncap the expensive purple marker
and smell its hue drain
each vivid molecule unzipping
like a train
simultaneously leaving and arriving
like gin on the tongue
at some auspicious seaport of the brain
where the cat burglar
raises the sash again for the
shush scene with the pillowcase
to scatter the jewels in light

Will you
retract the dewclaw
rewrap each silhouette
for maximum
frivolity and shrewdness
and land
like a cat on the lawn
sure as a lawn dart, a spear and a bee bee

which all have the same life purpose:

to make a bee-line

to point to the eye

to punctuate

improve it

a bank shot from childhood lawlessness

thrown into all possible futures

preserved in the aqueous humor

like eggs preserved in the pickling jar

or a cat in lemonade

whatever's barking in this scene

that's not the dog

is the cat

that's my gift to you

I will ride the Fragonard

-pink-slipper down the Fragonard

-throat of the frog

separate the black flies from their wings

I mean from flight

yet bring them into the true beauty

of their Latin names

Musca domestica and *Drosophila*

wingless but arm'd as if with beauty

maybe it's beauty maybe we can't tell

a lace mantilla and a breastplate

the large shell with a goddess in it

pressed on soap or pressed into a molded plastic

clamshell travel soap case that goes sick with

soppy soap and no travel—

I hate that limp print—

roll that up and drop it behind the fridge

ugh it might combust—fish it out again with a yardstick

flatten it out

put it somewhere safe

which is somewhere away from the eye

a further basement of a further banishment

the farthermost cornice of some farthermost room

inside inside

the corneal blue

your bridegroom rides away from and leaves you with

that key to the room that is your doom

lovely

let me lift that key from you

the reticulated scales of the spyglass

fit one into another

the more inside you go

the more gold and smaller

the golden fish

dunked in the river for her vanity

well, fish her out

too while we're at it and also

fish out the river from its bed

lock the eye itself

clapping for itself

with one hand with the other

clapping itself shut

the clock can't talk

because its mouth is full of pins

it looks on cross as a cat

gin and fizzy bitters

rise all around the green plot

the pilot rides his biplane by in the sky

clean as a nursery ceiling

unsinged

and while the sun thinkens in the yard

I'll take a yard of this

slit it with your egg tooth

I'm so sick of this place

but it's the only place

9.2.20

DAUGHTER STYLE

to order the black sneakers

to keep the late appointment
to convince the lady hygienist to see you
even now, even now when we're so late
large, glossy, and made of power
like Europa pulled away by cow to drown at sea
who comes back every morning as her avatar, Dawn
she leads you off to the white interior
your grin is spreading

it's so American to hurt you like this
for the sake of your own white teeth

to send the old pair back
to order the next size up
to study your toes, how they line up
shell-pink and auspicious
as Romanovs in snow

when I'm your age I sit in the schoolroom
and contemplate wheel of fortune
the cardboard globe tilts in its metal brace
if you pull it out of the brace it has two holes in it
and is easily dented

which is what the brace is for

but you have to dislodge it to learn this

so it's already too late

as we stare at the door

try to melt the afternoon with laser vision

tap at smashed screens with sore fingers

(you're with me now)

Will you

take back

what you said

if I swathe you

in denials

thick as a

sneaker tread

my own inutility

gapes like a snake in the stars

flashes fangs

writhes pointlessly

and swallows nothing

I don't bother to look up anymore

but grope under your pillow for devices

under the datestamp, a tsunami

battens then retracts from the amusement park

thinking better and leaving

a huge eye of wheel in the mud

in my mind's black eye,

an old nerve winks like a lost fortune

an old possibility goes gill-green

sneakers wash up along the shoreline

in your sleep you repeat the motion

of advancing, retracting

of flinging wide your nets to net the moon

but like every tide you fail

some mad duct is governing this

some mad derangéd government

tries to fit you into its business

so you draw red nets on your wrists

like a pulsing star you signal

like a star you fail to hide behind your signal

9.22.20

MARY SHELLEY

The cavity of air where the sea is missing
like a tooth wrenched clean at the root
we've taken lodgings in a harrow
a shirtwaist for my habiliment
and you always in your hood
zipped in, my little nitrogen fixer
your tubby pea-shaped abdomen
I lately feel a seacave
screaming
and a bone widens
temporally, tremens
but it comes to nothing
the sea doesn't even wait around to hear itself
percuss then rush out
the lung's hung with wet wool
its own shipwreck
and a throw of the dice can't alter its
inconsequence
nailbones rattle off the baize
and chalk sighs on the cue
we walk along the vaultbed
in bankers' visors
green: the strong breeze
has swept the field clean of toddlers

seabirds deposit

a litter of shit and shells

so you could mistake it

for a seabed

lit with a fleet

of geese who clear their throats

to indicate something indescribable

as they take to the sky

in a glottal paste

to elaborate their messaging

20,000 leagues over the sea

20,000 deck chairs

20,000 reading lamps

elaborately inverting

and wickering, clanking in the sky

don't look up or the tip

of the arrow will split you

the land dips and buckles

our socklings suckle and our soakings rot

in rubber

whose tread signifies two decades of bad luck

a so-far century's bad quintessence

crabs scuttle with their arms bent decorously

as if for a breakfast to be placed there

a breakfast at the courts of law!

a prayer breakfast

a scenic breakfast

a breakfast at the chemo suite

a working lunch

donuts outside the clinic before the protest

for all the fetuses must live to breed

and bustle for a groat

like goose or goat

feedbucket over handlebar

apron over gut

rosin over catgut

peruke over peruke

fabric fanfare that grips the livid throat

gullet that wants to rise

like a gilt bullet

in the breast pocket

in the waistcoat

in the opera box

the waistcoat

over the shirtwaist

the shirtwaist

over the waist

the waist

over another waist

over the green

lawn we trip and

hey presto

your signature

the glad

hand of fate

to gather here

in gooses

sup on swill

in sunlight

a second breakfast

a third

10.19.20

A DECAYING LEAF

three vital signs
rocket in green
one races, one stalls, one falls behind
like Keats's Indolence Ode
when he had taken a cricket ball to the eye
or like three little glyphs in a GIF
pitching a carloan, a houseloan, a schoolloan
to the part of my brain
that still knows this terminology:
delete it
       bicuspid brain
go back and eat pho in that glass box again
in the deserted mall
where steam streamed down the faces
in the line all down the mall
go back and leaf
through the calendar of wants
I kept but lost on purpose
after I thought I got what I wanted
when I want to look at it
I only have to scream

until my screamface sags
like a child's

when everything that can be done for it

has been done

I couldn't see it then

I couldn't see us cross the line

but the camera caught it

and when the image cycles by

it rips my brain out through my eyes

rip the seam out

stitch it shut

lift each instrument

smash it up

in her eightieth year

my mother achieves the goddess stage

performs her devout errand

of bargaining for things and

bringing them back

the eternal return to the half-dead mall

some of you owe a lot to death

and some of you own a little patch of death's floor

and some of you should refinance now

reach for more

open a line of credit

now while rates are low

and the discontinued

vacuum-cleaner bags list in their wire tier

like surplus saints in their sepulchre—
scoff the scoff of the defunct—

three plaster casts
of the dead infant's hand
rise like night flowers in the box
(the fourth one broke in the mold)
I hid the box
but now I dig it up
because I want to live in it
there where you rip
your steep error
all across my
bank of screens
across my lonely-throated station
where I count the banded warblers
tap the safety glass
and wait for the laws of heaven
to drop on me like a safe
two plaques that smack
two braids that smack the skull
as you round the bases
little girl you
shake and seize
your plastic beads
inside the batting helmet
your brain side and your smack side
beat beat your bicep

flexes for the sword and shield you will not

take up yet you sup

from a tube you

are good company but you

give nothing back

as you roll

like a coin

on the solar track

both sides bear your face

and both faces are masked

from minima to minima

the ain't of you

makes tracks

beat

it out of me

give it back

11.19.20

The serpentine taps my grown shoulder anymore
I mean the wind I'm not wearing no one wears anymore
It's made from the not-healthiest strands of hot feeling
melted down in the seventies when I learned to be grown
then a flammable flight of gins tilts and goes chin-chin
Datsun sunrise on the New Jersey side from the airport
estuary next to the cement plant carbon-
copy-colored-yellow-cigarette-smoked-drape
canary that smoked its last, and croaked—
         And even now when driving westward
along Gary's wastewater treatment plant
inexplicably Art Deco–domed
like a jelly mold on my left and a mill
drooling vaguely on the lakeface on my right
the way waste is sealed into barrels and hid
under ocean or mountain—it's gonna leak and rise
like a werewolf rises at night on his lotus
from his horrible locus
to kiss his mother the moon
I want her moonboots
her gloves that change colors
and her press-on nails for teens
I want to ride around in her coupe
let me be the rip of all this seam these guardrails

lead to the Burlington Coat Factory or Filene's

bucking and biting

for the desirable marked-down

factory second sheer propellant for each new brand of sheen

now the serpentine wind taps my shoulder

now the tap has run dry and the money has flown

maybe it'll come back to the coop when it's tired

like some weather-worn note in a seventies song

that crinkled green bill even now holds wisdom

spills its gust

from its stent

from its polyester vest

that's some lovely next-level revealed moon goddess magic

wrist flips to the B-side

and the dead rise on fishy footfalls

or a dead star falls this way not that

smashing or sparing a lickspittle pine forest

In the mirror universe of the women's dressing room

in the Kodak booth where the girls sit on stools

and huff developing chemicals

it's called a susurration, but I can't be sure

it's coming back this time tho time's

coming-back-from-commercial-break music

rings always now around the bleached-out flagpole's

exhausted

rush hour

rush the millrace by the onramp

the programming hole the water gap

where ducks have loose tongues to lap it

up loosefingered bunker hill wallpaper dawn

keeps nobody warm

not even an full-grown adult angora rabbit with a lap

band a bandolier or even

a lilac-colored quilted

careerwear overcoat belted over pearlseeded

rabbit mask will not prevent a rabbit war

gold wheat sheaf in formica chafing dish

party food miniaturized and peculiarly sheened

for the cookbook shoot

with gelatin

this book about rabbits

this clubdown you were thankful for

these cokes and these coke-bottle goggles agog

chemistry set all afire

this planet's chemical plant features

swollen bolusy over the airport

dusk swinging its flashlight

down into Liberty's eyes

her spiked visor

her drive to Vermont to peep leaves

with her lover, even now,

leatherette suitcase in the trunk with its buckle now

goodbye

New Jersey cosmos

you crooked team-time of my birth

adult ashtray wore its dream down to divorce

the lampshade was for lovers

your bumper sticker

coffeecup t-shirt

wanted life to be better

than it was

then it was

11.23.20

FIRST SNOW / "LIVE MUSIC
RETURNS TO THE GAZEBO"

First blood, first snow

live music returns to the gazebo

and I think it must coldly clatter there

and gather in the hexagonal vertices

impossible to determine now the scale of the scene

so far from its first happening

first feline whipcars of snow

first catlike swoosh of the Jordans

entering air

as the midshipman neighbor

matriculates at the warcollege

for every lady arm must bear its lamp

and every war its matrices

wide eggy solar notes

come flooding the zone

up to the gym rafters

spilling and lowing

out to where

the high school choir

clambers up on risers

inside the gazebo

to sing and watch the snow burn

what's not divine

is cut out and thrown in the river

the mortal part

must be cut away

so only the god remains

as the hymn separates from the choir

what makes it holy

what coldly gathers

freon, neon and ozone

cans of concentrate

revolve in the atmosphere

clattered by solar wind

and all the brothers who can't sing

come careening like oxen

with the trunk of a sacred oaktree

snowchained to their trunks

come swift or come struggling

down to the gazebo

which appears to have lifted off

just in time

or is it an illusion

caused by the risers

that lift the teen choir

red scarves stretch stiffly from their throats

like thought bubbles and speech bubbles

the lengthy watchman's report

that relates the catastrophe

and thereby spares us the expense of staging it

I climb up to the roof to watch the scene

a splinter buries itself in the quick of my thigh

I carry it with me always

a charm of bad endings and nerve endings

carillons back through the decades

through Novocaine and iodine

freon, neon, and ozone

a needle always pointing away

to the agonal gazebo

in the cleaned-out noumenal park

hosed clean of crowds and evidence

of ought but snow and tennis business

and cleanliness itself

and cold

grows sharper and more concentrate

till it pricks awake the sleeping toddler

who rises in his crib

and kicks the wall

to illustrate

how a dreamcat was freed from a hole

then the dreamwall breaks

then the gazebo tumbles out

and goes flying through the air

like a cat kicked clean of wall

and vomits up a comet as it goes

and saturates the scene

with fang

and firstblood

and livemusic

12.8.20

THE BLONDES

Even on this cold plump date I see above me

a vision of a maiden bleeding from the septum—I mean a
teen dream

with ironed hair streaking flatly away—up the sightline

of a schoolgirl with her sharp chin pointing up

a cold sheer nasal corridor canting steeply away from us

wherein you could squint to make out an uppermost crack

where in wind could blow like light

and manifest trashily

trash that can leave and be swept up on wind

we so devoutly wanted

to leave and be swept up in

get trashy

and ultimate

on the high vinyl mat left out behind the highjump

where the track edged on some kind of shaggy nursery

baking there abandonedly

swoop of sun-in can't lift the hair too dark for it

picking plastic shredded coating off the paperback

temporary perfection

via an array of inhalable minipoisons

like a bat this vision materializes out of the morning

to swoop in the long hallway of the school

an inky penstroke, stroke sequelae on a scan

a brighter version of the wind

to sling a book at and bring down

first I was hit by the door then the doorjamb

then I came in swinging

in the basement the band rotated like junk saints

in the garage some guy blinked then touched two wires together

cured in the formaldehyde of our collapsible classroom

we ran out on the mesa to watch the storm arrive

I lay down on the picnic table and let my braids drain

and the live oaks rise

I lay down lithe in the edison bulb

and took the current

ethelrosenberg

ethylalcohol

ethelcalledsusie

my first cousin's name

and once removed

it was a youthful fantasie, starring me, a neverblonde

the whole smashed-up edition of the faerie queen

reverted to pulp soaked in vodka in the gut

onlie to arise again on the gullet

of a depressive aromatic lady voter

also me

with a sash around my waist with a loaf

of stolen stollen on my arm

for gods above a gloating Wotan

the glabrous gold sigil of the Wu-Tang clan

dozing on its flagstaff

practiced attitudes of dismay my resting expression

and yes it rose that way

and froze

my face

the clapper of the poppet in the clock

resting by the quarter hour

smiling for nobody in the dark

when the weathergirl arrives

(her miniskirt, her ironed hair)

each task or commitment

explodes its combustible husk

in the flare-y sudden cargo of the truck—

       it took me getting hi-lo

it took me turning that dial this way and that

it took me crashing that truck

it took me getting this dent in my brow

it took me getting my head caved in

it took me cashing in my accounts

it took me getting clocked like this

it took me wearing the deep cleft around

like the hoofprint of the aleph-ox

or the bird's back when its wings are spread

or any other suggestive and aromatic cleft

it took me turning my ear to it

to struggle for signal

unhasping my jaw and discarding it

it took me fumbling with the fillet knife

my knuckles frozen in the rime

on the shipboard cannery

between gigs as a student and a sea instructor

with my bowie knife and my ghillie knife

it took me being this one grainy stripe of white

in the muscle

just one briefly knotted tendentious stripe

easier to cut

away

than this cold semisolid oracular feeling

that is both liquid and more-than-ice

some kind of incredible mind-stage sluicing through

from the ambiguity of god-language

to flood the mucky guts that flood the deck

with the certainty

of doing something wrong of doing something wrong

eightminutes for the water to boil

alphabet noodles for the kids' soup

or whatever returns to earth

whatever needs to come back here

to earth

has eight minutes

Mr Sunshine

whatever we hurled up into the troposphere

has to return

any weather arriving

any messenger from the gods

when we thought we were through with it—

any invisible chemical soupiness that

smelled like cleanliness and

spelled out drastic riddles

in the drain

melting baby sock in the dryer

becoming particulate

entering air

and entering art

and telling no secrets

and going nowhere

then raining back down again like a clockwork

for the baby to inhale

like everything that ran down around my ankles to tell me

in the rightness of that concentrated cold

the coldness of garbage swilling in the gutters

money seemed to need an icehouse, a bank to live in

but really it was everywhere and nowhere at once

like that god who couldn't commit

but rained gold sometimes when he felt like it

who you were always fucking in the shower

1.6.21

MOMS OF THE UNDERWORLD

"Unable to resolve this riddle/I died of remorse."

That was the day
        I turned on me
my sphinx face.

I was proud of the claw, the tail, the wing
        and the scales that marked me as every well-defended
monster and fortress

in one. I tossed my mane.
        My naked breasts could be overlooked (by me)
as they grinned like armed brigands from my chest.

Keeping watch for what
        I peered out the portals
where no photons reached.

My photoreceptors
        dozed like missiles
on their pads. At my snout

spread white smoke
        a sinking shirt on waves.
Each hole hid a hole

where a buried cable
        telegraphed the brain
-wet meadow, also strewn with holes

where a gilt-hooved cow might turn her heel
        or an agile girl her ankle as she turned into a cow
or turned to take the full weight of the bull

-ground that wears a winter scurf all spring
        drags it all around the spaceship or town
wears it all the way down.

Something is failing here
        on the organelle level
the two living children

the dead one the girl
        who never knew the weather
outside me that broke

me what a joy to know now
        what she's missing as I
order every living thing down

on its knees
        to scumble in the mud
for pomegranate seeds

1.8.21

ON THE HOODED MERGANSER,
THAT CLOCK-FACED DUCK

A black-bordered letter

    arrives from your mother

        I mean mother-me, the mother duck

who rides on river

    pulls up her hood

        to deliver the letter

(the hood and the letter a

    -re made of the river)

        —you gonna swim in this river,

you gotta take off that sweatshirt

    you've been wearing forever.

        —you mean the only thing holding me

up or together?

    As a paper egg

        dissolves on water

I cried for my mother

    when died my bright lyre

        at eyerise the thought of her

steams thru the ether

    like a yolk in its vapor

        consumes its own sulphur

leaves that duck-egg-green aura

    on the brow of dawn

        and yet I still see

83

from my blind in the river

        that bright broken boat tow

          drives only away

which shoreline or eyesore

      now should I row for

           now with my army-green

feathers in sweatshirt

        like a stormfront from heaven

           wears flagrags in mud

the sewer runs straight

        from grate to the gut

          of the river this leadshot

 in duckbrain

       can't sup

         can't drain

can't learn the names of your mother

        from before you were born

          can't speak them from inside the egg

if it doesn't want to be born

        but rolls away to hide its face

          like a dime or duck stuck

in a coinslot or grate

       this sweatshirt bird

         can't go can't stay

can't dawn

     fold her arms around

         her egg around her day

2.8.21

MARY MAGDALENE,
COLLECTIBLE GLASSES

like a fop I arrived

at dawn to the ward

my watch fob on my vest

chained like a bird at my breast

as if a bird could be a shield against Time's advance

a bullwark against Time's

consequence

a bullword drew closer

above the doctor's head

took the shape of a cloud

tried to omenize the future

tried to piss it out like rain

as the doctor dragged the bed between us

and launched bad news across it

I watched the soundcloud

flood the port and then arrive

all out of order

a swelling cloud, a swelling tide

a crowd a chord

some welling that could fill a room

then capsize

I was the room or in it

tho I comprehendeth it not

like when I arrived

to the dell at dawn

to find my lover gone

from his grave in the cave

my eye tongued the hole

in the roof of the mouth

of the thought blown back

from the blast of that thought

the rock aghast

glastnost at last

a collectible glass

for each unsurfeitable

fountain of coke

hung shattered in the air

in dropletted burden

· one minute past

I went agape and agog

I imitated the rock

but comprehendeth not

I imitated the rock

but comprehendeth not

as soda flew without stopping

from the side of the rock

it grew a little bitter

and a little more bad

each day as two drains

flew like buttresses

down from the baby's gut

as devils flee heaven

or an eightpound goth

-ic cathedral where bad news rose

through a gothic rose

window then changed

to a cloud and rained

on every baby's breath in the glade

bent down all under the welter

weight of water each fox

-bell went under each petaled

human humhum lumen

-lantern thus snuffed out

a bad deal I drank down

with my hands in my mouth

I imitated the clown

who imitated the mouse

who lived in the clock

like it said in the song

I was right twice a day

marched out and struck

myself in the face

the rest of the time

I imitated the drain

I did the limited-edition

imitation drain

3.13.21

I'm sick of writing the word *ghost*
sick of the silent *h*
the most rotten luck and the most rotten faith.
The children are tucked up in bed like in *Medea*
that is, crouched behind the roofridge and ready to rise
with their mom on the machina
tricked out in flame.
The fridge motor whines.
Everything whines
like the moon when the big hand points to twelve
and the plot arrives
and a fleet of police choppers rise up in the sky.
They want to ride away from their crimes
unlike Medea
who spells hers out on the sky
in milk that rots and smells.
She carries her dead kids like whelks in a bucket
and everybody knows
how charred flesh falls back to show the bone
but nobody knows
why the river rolls back
to upchuck what's dunked
there like a drunk
hatchback
with its headlights on.

The river just likes it that way

and the river's like, open your eyes.

Why is that

river mud

so dirty and so right.

I'm getting tired of the *h* in *river*

sorry I mean *ghost* I mean the fridge light you write by

well you paid for it now

you gotta lie

down in a bed in a dress that's too tight.

The sight of money

draining in the sink

then I hocked

then I hurled

then I upchucked the Voyager

all the way out into space

like a hatchback

with its lights on

and the baby-on-board sign on board

to upload its payload of sound

into the clouds

someplace else.

ha! ha!

The h in catastrophe

sticks to the p

like a stray cat limps around the block

with one paw up.

Medea's kids get restless

need to eat, need to pee.

Every once in awhile their little faces show above the roofline.

Mother thou has slain me they mewl

under their milkbreaths

waiting to be picked up.

They pace around

run the zippers of their tracksuits

up and down.

Meanwhile moonlight slicks the payphones

with desolate glamour

the metal umbilical cords and

dark receivers.

Meanwhile I'm so furious and meanwhile

you're so young

you think you can hide

what you stole from me

beneath your pillow

—I'm looking at it right now—

where your crossed arms cradle

your sleeping head.

4.23.21

POINT BREAK

How the sea is
always stunting for the camera
a cat's paw always scumbling for a mouse
I wanted to write about Sound
without hearing, noise
-less heart-throb slotting carefully into the sine
waves like
an FBI file in its drawer: go
on, lie, skydive, surf,
rob, gaze, flick your good hair
out of the way as if your cheekbones
could slice your own face.
The lady director says
The lady director the
lie detector
sends me reeling and
rootling over seaface like a sow
ripping it up.
                    Eyelevel cuts
in styro, eye in the hambone, hyoid
muttle snapped in a strankle, impetigo'd
wrestling mat that empurpled the cheek
of every older brother on the team. Things
you might do with a daughter

to break the gods' embargo on travel and

maketh the winds to rise:

The seashore rolls white with dead fishfat,

adipose, in the concrete

washroom where you peel down the wet suit and the chlorine

rises to hug the sinuses like a shower of girls, oh, the sestet

sneezes, the octet bloats its stopp'd flute

a fed-up bellows goes phoo-phoo

and Beauty goes off somewhere else to get stuffed

up the flue

like, I'm Etna,

fuming, maternal, settled, and mad:

about to unleash on all of you a killing mud

but I'm also distracted by a shipscene where a cat

slops brains and guts

shortens the time to factory like a god pleased

with what rises on the wind: what: strange stink

like a pop song sticks to matter or the Sound of her respirators

Compressors, I guess. Motors.

thanks so much. And the two drains that hung

from her gut.

Thanks.

The nurses say

Art is long

but I fear they have that wrong

I want to be

gutted and fed to the shipboard cat

or swept harmlessly into the sea to break down and caress

the calfskin where Keanu

spills from the vents

jeeps out to catch a sick and then

falls from the sky trailing silk for

all these stunts are fake

but not all of them *all these stunts*

were faked in heaven

as the missing canister of film blows open

it projects on the interior of the bus

(like a bower Keats would've built for us)

that mote-degraded scene

where Keanu paddles *backwards* into the surf

and falls apart into the sea

oxen garland

the daughter-welcoming sea

5.6.21

TERMINATOR 2, LATE STYLE

I want that green possibility
the gravidity of late style
pregnant with self-possession
to spring me to the end of the plot
Meanwhile I dream of Iphigenia
and how many times that teen can drop
in her altar top
When my teens are doing nothing
they are doing dance moves off TikTok
their brainwaves altering
like the ones with wands
who wave the planes down
and meanwhile I blow too much
dough on the baby's summer
clothes. Oh
well, if he wears it just once*
(*in the grave), then it's worth it.
I say the secret thought
in my brain like a spark
It lays down and snuffs
in the mossbane of the earbone.
It dies a crib death.
Bring me my toy stethoscope. No,
I can detect nothing. Two beer cans

on a cord? No. Radio silence.

Come in. Do you read me. No.

Wish I was done

like the LA River, put to bed,

maybe light up again by moonlight.

As a teen I watched Terminator 2

about the mom so strong she hurled

an eighteenwheeler sideways down the riverbed

to lift her teen

on the shockwave. It was the only way

she could reach him.

What would that look like now

if I had the right device, what angel

would answer the landline

of that bad idea if I went scrambling with a branch

up the dome of heaven

to scribble my bad vow.

VEIL OF ERROR. Poor sow,

born with all your eggs in your basket

wish I took better

care before I went rootling up the interior

all the husks up with my tusks,

stampling down the shells.

That's just arithmetic:

you have so much time & then you run out:

rain rains stops and losses, the soffit rots

& floods the roof. Call the roofer. Meanwhile,

one man's half-minotaur,

and so more man than ox, while the other's

half-bucentaur, so twice oxen.

When speaking of men

one half finds a way

to be bigger. The roofer

won't come. The state barge

goes rolling down the levy

with its balls between its wheels

for the Wedding of Venice

to the Sea. Wild flowers

in the burn plane

form a swoosh

you can see from space

while the wood runs out

in the crematoria.

You have to help them out.

You have to lift the state barge of Venice

in your mom-arms

and send it caroming

down the LA River

till it reaches the end of the plot.

Spring in flames, an eighteenwheeler

& Iphigenia. The dead can't help you.

You have to help them out.

CONCLUSIVE DEATH STYLE:

A KATABASIS FOR RIVER PHOENIX

I am speaking now of the tower

scoliotic, sclerotic

over streets that slanted steeply

like a sick and listing ship

How it flagged like a flower

yet could still point to a star

and suck dye up its vasculature

like any schoolkid knows

how to fashion a crude siphon

from a tube, a tank, a parked car

and, of course, your mouth.

Meanwhile, you go down

with hemophilia

and the guards switch sides

till we're all down in the basement

watching a movie on a sheet

and this movie's a two-reeler

and it's kind of a two-hander

and it's kind of a tear-jerker

and it's kind of the production of a serious sentimentalist

and it's starring two stars one light one dark

the blue expanse is just a tacky backdrop

compared with these two

and you're the light one
you're the star
who left the light on
all night and burnt out

your pompadour rises
as if from a bomb test
alarmed and expansive
knocking it all out
there's not a lot of thinking here
there's not a lot of light
there's not a lot going on
I'd prefer to lie and die outside the viper room
with all my friends suspended on the shockwave
as on the red and black walls of Greek vessels
or burst petechiae in the eyewalls
as on TV the victim strangles
oh shut up well anyway any
picture is possible
any urn at all

and it's not particularly sweet to remember
how you tapped your ash
how you knocked your cherry off
how I wanted to leap off the bridge with you
but lost my contact lens in the grass
it was such expensive plastic
I had to drive home with one eye

open

and behind me

the other

that perfect lens

in the grass

the eye that god made for me

so I could image his face

and yours as you ashed

your Marlboro there

you ashed it from the trainbridge

the drifting of a god

the drifting of gold

in a river

when ever after

the river

was dragged by

divers

you only turned up

later elsewhere

you only turned up

your face

River I'm trying to see around you

to an idea of art

that's both pit and tower

dick and uterus at once

inside the blood can splash, replenish

and shed all over again

piss heat and daylight

invert to a flock of bats

fly back

and hang close

irritatingly loyal

isn't consciousness like that though

I'd love to slough off

the lining of thought

from the wall where bats scuff

like schoolshoes

and about that big

and there's plenty here

plenty of nothingness

plenty of height

and plenty of lowliness

and plenty of dark

plenty of no

odors but our own

and nothing

but the furs we wore in life

derealizing into odor

our sightlines sharpening in our skulls

that look on nothing

our vision

admittedly

and at last improved

to you I can say

I refuse
to shut my eyes
because I was robbed
of something
by a god
and I'm going
to keep looking
till I find it.

AGONY IN THE GARDEN

for my son

AGONY IN THE GARDEN

BEGINNING AND ENDING WITH A TWEET FROM NYC COMBINED SEWERS

§

raw sewage runs down to Coney Island Creek
as the baby sleeps
a seraph slips
in through a slot in the zoetrope
to learn what it's like
to wink at the world from the inside

§

as ribbons of milk run
down from the baby's hungopen mouth
to wreathe his hairline
and dry there, a lactic crown
the zoetrope
turns on her axis
for the umpteenth time tonight
and all kinds of fraudulent shadows arise

§

bad news, lil dude. lily badge
on your baby breast identifies you
as human, requiring oxygen. galactic
monsoons crow at creekrise
raw sewage runs down to Coney Island Creek
from a donor creek
and one bank leans on its sister bank and sighs

§

a revolver
picks a slug from a sampler of blanks
—lunar, ochre, samphire—
where Bellerophon's hoof struck the rock
white cheesy fever flowers flew out forever
and raced like cats for the moon

§

as a cheese is named for its rind
so the daughter for her mother
the ewe for her dam
the fan for her fancam
the wire for her splitter
so whatever arrives on two feet
splits or shits in the river

§

accept my prophecy
it's dangerous to sleep

§

when you twist the strings
you see the bird escape its cage
but it's stuffed back inside
when you lay the toy aside

§

creek
-bed, moonbed, dime you turn
on yourself you turn
on the security firm's

110

silent alarm
dim night hums
a current converts
the limestone lobby
into a tank of green light

§

we look so good in the closed circuit let's
knock this bank over forever
crack the vault
go on vaulting
way up in the sky
everywhere we go the glow
of fame shall
follow us like the smoke that rises
from the vest stitched with blanks
in the scene where we're shot apart

§

but no
light breaks as good as they
look tonight
sleeping in the garden
as their boss prays
and the soldiers approach
their cloaks
ride up to show
italicized
hairy thighs

§

in this painting called *Agony
in the Garden*
by Andrea Mantegna

§

as fistfuls of tickertape leap
down to the street
and run off to Coney Island Creek the raw
footage gives the Pathé rooster
something to cry about
and the siren that rides
the cop car
slumps in its reluctant
crop of curls
and cries

§

lucid, illicit
dust rides a motebeam
down to nothing where nothing
lifts its white sheet
to catch the image like a baby soon
dawn
will let one slutty ray
slip through a slit in her robe
                    as if dawn could
shoot vision like a burst
of milk from her tit
                    as if dawn goes on
mincing and
dribbling from the mouth of day
all night

§

(for vision is
truly a bitch
and consciousness a
toy
            a zoetrope)

§

or day from the mouth of dawn
spills whose bleach-blonde curls
part like champagne
from the mouth of Marie
Antoinette falls open as she sleeps
who staged it that way
built an Alp for the sun to come up on
like a shepherdess she that
blonde kind of sleep

§

when the nurse rinses the baby's hair
I'm struck as by a bullet
train or beam
milk runs from the rock of my breast
champagne runs down the creek
of the sink

§

the secret lies
in Coney Island Creek
you'll learn the true cost
when the bill arrives
congratulations
on your destruction
you with your mouth
full of sand and samphire
stuck in the ruts of your teeth

§

trash blows
from the mouth of the cave
smoking wore a hole there
in the lapel of the Rose

her mouth slipping open
her robe
a mouth for ghosts
girth of snow unloosed from its storehouse
the snowplow keeps coming by lowering its tusks
waking the baby up well let it
                              why don't you
it's still a union job

§

this blender
has no dimmer
only off-on

§

I learned scripture from the bleachers
peering into my debts
on a TV above a bar in Pennsylvania

§

for Mantegna loved mankind enough
to paint them at the most awkward angles
and let them still look pretty hot
fixed like a punk's bangs in egg tempera
so much attention
lavished in such strange directions

§

who nuzzled the muzzle
who set a rooster's egg
rolling down the slot
of a bad day
who
hobbled by on trotters

that day you
learned the name of all the beasts

§

derecho
sinister
tributary
bursary
the backdrop is serene
while the lit-up
proscenium arch
collapses like a bank

§

wind comes tumbling down the hole
wind winds back into it
on windy nights the reception goes out
in the middle of the game
static supplies the crowdsound
raw sewage runs down to Coney Island Creek
snow spikes the football
pelts the earth with love

§

I greet you from the middle
of a shitty relationship
or maybe slightly nearer to the end
though I am looking good
through the hole in your foot
up at the dog of you
laid out on the bed

§

like the dog I am

a dog at the deposition

§

a place to hide
w/ a hole in the wall for your money
in your hospital gown and
collapsing oakleave crown you nincompoop the microscop
-ic herbivary
in the gut
snowmill of consciousness
capacious winding sheet
requiring extraction
takes exception
to the puzzling pharmacopia sewn into the ground

§

with blue black stitches
like the coroner or the psychopath sews up your eyes
anywhere I strike I
rest my case

§

gladiator sandals come back into vogue
raw sewage runs down to Coney Island Creek
and everything rises on its bilge
jubilation
turns out to be awful
who will answer for this
who seeded the cosmos with iron
so I could be born and
turn to watch you
go under
as I'm yanked up out of the tank

§

I scatter my notes
on a galax that has more iron
-y than just
-ice the hand that falls open or
closes in sleep
is a tsar's tumbrel
a rooster's egg loaded with spores
is tumbling hair
in the mare's nest galaxy
an omen and a prodigy
brought low now to earth

§

now release her
cartwheeling across the sky
an electrified cat
on a billboard
bestride the sideshow
with her black tail on fire
and her claws in the muck
let curl from her mouth
a curl of light from a locket
booster rocket or shot in the thigh
shoot it up and let it fall
back in the sky
go thick and viscid down dark channels
where the light has gone
when it's gone all night
as wind is in the wire
baby's watching TV
raw sewage runs down
to Coney Island Creek

AFTERWORD

Repetition, I have come to understand, is the shape trauma makes of time.

After we lost our daughter, I wanted time to not just stop, but to repeat. Even if I couldn't have a different ending, I wanted to have those thirteen days with her again. I was caught in a problem impossible to solve. How could I reconcile grief's desire to look backwards with survival's command to move forward in time, towards a future where I didn't much want to go?

To endure this contradiction, and to study my own endurance, I wrote *Death Styles*. I set myself three rules. First, I had to write daily. Second, I had to accept any inspiration presented to me as an artifact of the present tense, however incidental, embarrassing or fleeting (these are identified as the subtitles for the poems). Third, I had to fully follow the flight of that inspiration for as far as it would take me. I had to tolerate the poem for the time it took to get it down.

I wrote these poems largely in our Rust Belt backyard, an odd, narrow lot braced by chainlink and weeds. When the wind changed the weather, all the ailing trees ducked their heads and turned up pale leaves marked with black round fungus, like a cigarette burn in a palm. I thought of harm, and of *hamartia*, the flaw in the hero's fuselage that brings him crashing to earth; I thought of the leaves that spilled from the mouth of the sibyl's cave, how her petitioners had to scramble to gather them up, and I felt grief for how hard we mortals have to struggle just to understand what is happening to us.

I am grateful to Ingeborg Bachmann, to whose unfinished trilogy my title refers. I am grateful to Bernadette Mayer, Hannah Weiner, Mary Shelley, Alice Notley, Kim Hyesoon, Dolores Dorantes, and all the lares and penates of the cosmic and the daily, for being with me as I wrote this book.

This book is for my living children.

ACKNOWLEDGMENTS

The poems of *Death Styles* appeared, in various guises, in the following venues: *Annulet, Bomb Magazine, Broadkill Review, Brooklyn Rail, Chicago Review, Fence, Fonograf, Gulf Coast, Indianapolis Review, Indiana Review, Kenyon Review, Lana Turner, Poetry Daily, Poetry Magazine...* and the marquee of the Ace Hotel in Los Angeles. I'm grateful to the editors and instigators who brought this to pass.

I'm also grateful to the friends and writers who saw me through the strange era of this writing—Johannes Göransson, Kate Bernheimer, and Kate Marshall—and to those who helped it into book form, including the gallant Jacques de Spoelberch and, of course, the glamorous editors and staff at Nightboat.

The completion of this book was supported by a Guggenheim Fellowship, the Shelley Memorial Prize from the Poetry Society of America, and a Literature Fellowship from the American Academy of Arts and Letters. I am grateful to the committees who selected me for these recognitions and to the staff of these institutions for their kindness and their time.

& Arachne—

Further in Summer than the Birds

Joyelle McSweeney is the author of ten books of poetry, prose, plays, and criticism. Her first book, *The Red Bird,* inaugurated the Fence Modern Poets Series in 2001; three more genre-flexing books—*The Commandrine and Other Poems, Flet,* and *Percussion Grenade*—were also published by Fence, while her short story collection *Salamandrine, 8 Gothics* and novel *Nylund, the Sarcographer* were published by Tarpaulin Sky. In 2012, her play *Dead Youth, or, the Leaks,* was selected to inaugurate the Leslie Scalapino Prize for Women Performance Artists and was published by Litmus Press. In 2014, McSweeney's *The Necro-pastoral: Poetry, Media, Occults,* an influential work of decadent ecopoetics, was published by the University of Michigan Poets on Poetry Series. 2020 saw the publication of the double poetry collection *Toxicon and Arachne* from Nightboat Books, which earned McSweeney the Shelley Memorial Prize from the Poetry Society of America, a fellowship from the American Academy of Arts and Letters, and a Guggenheim Fellowship. McSweeney is a co-translator of *Yi Sang, Selected Writing,* which received numerous recognitions, including the 2021 Aldo and Jeanne Scaglione Prize for Translation from the MLA. With Johannes Göransson, she is a co-founder of Action Books, an international press which has built readerships for major and emerging poets from around the world while centering translators and the act of translation itself. McSweeney is a Professor of English at the University of Notre Dame.

NIGHTBOAT BOOKS

Nightboat Books, a nonprofit organization, seeks to develop audiences for writers whose work resists convention and transcends boundaries. We publish books rich with poignancy, intelligence, and risk. Please visit nightboat.org to learn about our titles and how you can support our future publications.

The following individuals have supported the publication of this book. We thank them for their generosity and commitment to the mission of Nightboat Books:

Kazim Ali • Anonymous (8) • Mary Armantrout • Jean C. Ballantyne • Thomas Ballantyne • Bill Bruns • John Capetta • V. Shannon Clyne • Ulla Dydo Charitable Fund • Photios Giovanis • Amanda Greenberger • Vandana Khanna • Isaac Klausner • Shari Leinwand • Anne Marie Macari • Elizabeth Madans • Martha Melvoin • Caren Motika • Elizabeth Motika • The Leslie Scalapino - O Books Fund • Robin Shanus • Thomas Shardlow • Rebecca Shea • Ira Silverberg • Benjamin Taylor • David Wall • Jerrie Whitfield & Richard Motika • Arden Wohl • Issam Zineh

This book is made possible, in part, by grants from the New York City Department of Cultural Affairs in partnership with the City Council, the New York State Council on the Arts Literature Program, and the National Endowment for the Arts.